The Return of Rex and Ethel

WRITTEN BY

Arnold Adoff

ILLUSTRATED BY

Catherine Deeter

HARCOURT, INC.

San Diego   New York   London

Library of Congress Cataloging-in-Publication Data
Adoff, Arnold.
The return of Rex and Ethel/by Arnold Adoff; illustrated by
Catherine Deeter.
p.   cm.
Summary: Two girls who share many wonderful times with their beloved
dogs, Rex and Ethel, find a special way to remember them when they die.
[1. Dogs—Fiction.   2. Grief—Fiction.]   I. Deeter, Catherine, ill.   II. Title.
PZ7.A2616Re   2000
[Fic]—dc20   91-23397
ISBN 0-15-266367-3

First edition
A C E F D B

Printed in Hong Kong

The illustrations in this book were done in acrylics on
Strathmore illustration board.
The display type was set in Fontesque.
The text type was set in Kennerley by R&S Book Composition,
San Diego, California.
Color separations by Bright Arts Ltd., Hong Kong
Printed by South China Printing Company, Ltd., Hong Kong
This book was printed on totally chlorine-free Nymolla Matte Art paper.
Production supervision by Stanley Redfern and Pascha Gerlinger
Designed by Ivan Holmes

This book   is for our   own true dogs:
            Right here   or   over there
                          on   green ground
                          or   in   still   air
                          above our heads:
With   all   great   love.

                          —A. A. & C. D.

In our town   there is a quiet street   that runs to the edge of open fields
and a line of black walnut trees. There are two houses
close to each other,   with a large shared yard between,
and a broken-down fence   through the middle   of   that   yard.

In each house   there are families   and shelves filled with books   and carved
wood animals.   There are beds and tables,   and   refrigerators
filled with milk cartons   and   sweet   red   apples.

In each house   lives a young girl.   The girls are the best of friends.
Each girl has a dog.

The friends   are Pepper and Belle   and they have been neighbor girls
all   of their   long-legged   lives.
The dogs   are Rex and Ethel   and they have been neighbor dogs
all   of their   short-legged   lives.
The girls play with each other   and with   their dogs.
The dogs play with each other   and with   their girls.

In our town   there are two girls   and two dogs   and they are always
t o g e t h e r .

In the middle of their shared yard   each girl has built a doghouse
up against that old wood fence.   It has broken slats   and sagging sections.
There is an open gate with rusted   hinges   and a missing latch.

Pepper and Belle   grow up together during these years
of growing trees   and the open gate.   The girls go to school,
and come home to their families.   They talk and argue,   hug and sulk,
share granola bars   and moments of red apples.

And Rex and Ethel, the friend dogs, grow up together during years of training wheels and after-supper snacks. Rex and Ethel run and follow. They sit very still with their two girls, long into years of afternoons after school: into summer months of rest and play.

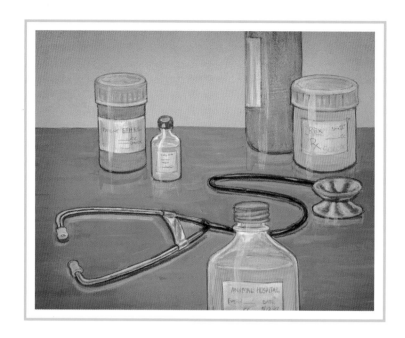

This summer, the girls celebrate their latest birthdays and are busy away from home most of the long hot days. They go to day camp at the town pool, for swimming lessons and wet fun.

Rex and Ethel stay in the shade of a black walnut tree. At their last visit to the animal clinic, the doctor talks about dog years, and dog knee joints: and the final power of old age and summer heat on dog livers and dog hearts.

Their short legs stiffen on cool mornings. And it is hard to even walk down the street with Pepper and Belle, for ice cream in deep paper dishes.

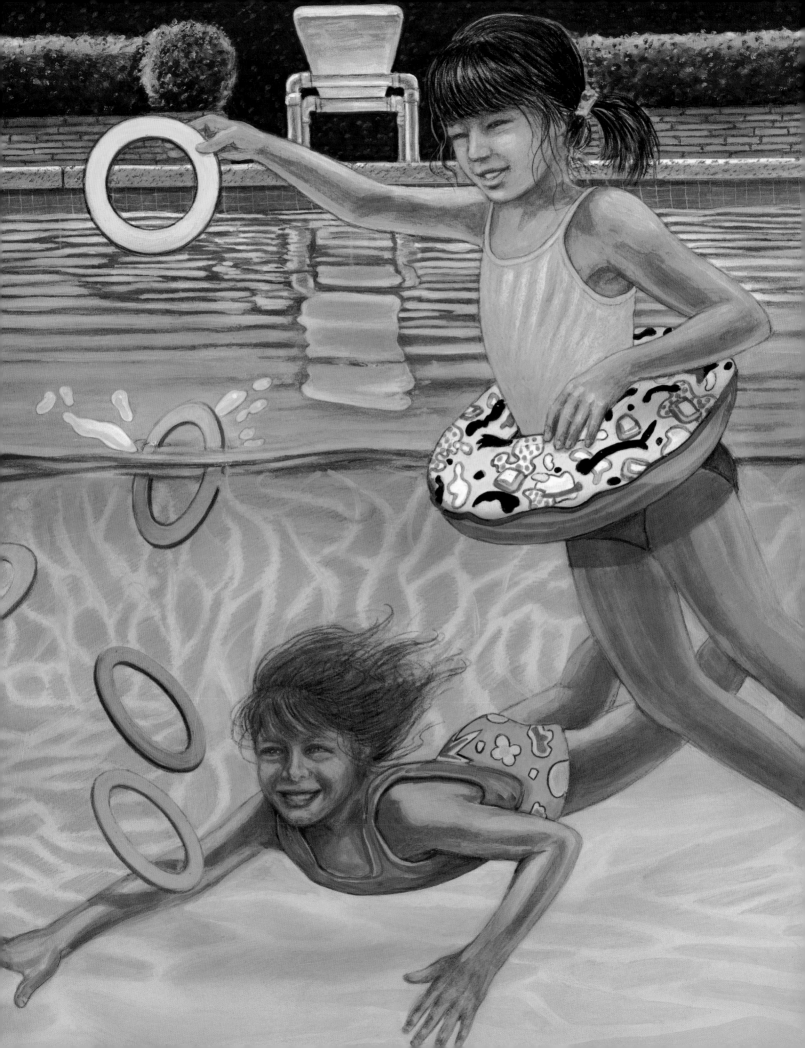

The girls place fresh straw and pieces of an old rug into each doghouse. They leave bowls of water and tidbits of food before they run to catch their bus each morning.

But the dogs don't eat much, these hot weeks, and stay in their cool houses, or in walnut tree shade.

One morning   at the end of August   the heat   seems   to   rise
out of the ground   to meet the rays of sun   beaming a   power
almost strong enough to cook yards of people and animals
into some soft August jelly.   The air   almost   breaks   into bits
of shimmering thin glass.

Both old dogs, Rex and Ethel, leave their doghouses and walk
slowly to the end of the fence. Side by side in tree shade
they lie panting, eyes opening and closing through the long day.

When the girls return from the pool, they drop their stuff and cool
their faces: one in her kitchen sink, one in her bathroom.
They run out their back doors, wet-faced and shouting, along the fence
to the line of trees.

The yard seems so very still. The air around their houses seems
to have run out of room: is hard to breathe.

Pepper and Belle find Rex and Ethel quiet on the ground, side by side
in the afternoon shade. Their bellies are not moving: so very still.

Now   each girl runs to her house   shouting for mothers and fathers
       to come and help.   There are hugs and tears.   There are old
       stories   of good times: of   years.
Now   both families gather at the trees.   They find a   flat
       soft space under shade   and begin to dig,   until a   large
       and deep   hole   is clear.

Now   Rex and Ethel are wrapped in old white sheets   and their pieces
       of   rug.   Parents help Pepper and Belle lower their dogs
       into the deep place.
Now   rawhide bones   and rubber balls that belong to each   are   placed
       with each.   Loose dirt and stones are added
       until the hole is full.

Now   they collect   heavy   flat stones   to place on the new grave.
Now   they rake   the loose dirt   and push down
       hard on the heavy stones.

Now Pepper and Belle cut away the hard green husks from some
of the walnuts lying on the ground. They push them between
the flat stones into the soft dirt.

Now walnut saplings will grow between these stones in new seasons.
Years of growing trees will join under the ground
with years of Rex and Ethel.

Now Pepper and Belle join hands with all in a circle around
this new space in the trees. Their eyes look down at fresh dirt.
Their eyes look up into evening sky. There is the cool smell
of coming rain that dries their warm wet faces.

Now it is getting dark. The ceremony is over. The two girls
hug each other hard. It is time to go
in for the night.

The next day is Saturday. The morning sun shines its full power
through the clear sky. There is time for cereal and sliced banana:
raisins   and   cookies   in each pocket.

The girls meet. They walk and ride their bikes along familiar
streets, to the highway at the edge of town. They talk about the
night before. They share pieces of nighttime dreams.

They go past dogs in their houses and yards, panting in the
still air of hot August. They go past cats sliding along old fences
and around bushes below bird feeders. They go past chipmunks
zigging into brush piles and under fallen logs. They see squirrels
tightrope-dancing along high branches to their leafy nests.

Pepper and Belle see stray dogs running free in the open fields.
A groundhog rises onto its hind legs. Geese are resting on the long
lawn by the big pond, their heads tucked down into downy chests:
in cool shade. They stir at the sound of bicycle tires on gravel,
and waddle into water.

Beyond the fields and into the woods, the girls see hints of
larger animals: running deer, and the flash of a red fox.
Along the road are the usual worms and crickets, and small green
snakes. Butterflies circle their heads.

And here and there along the side of the road are
animals hit by cars and run over: knocked to the blacktop edge.
A beautiful black skunk and a long-tailed squirrel lie side by side
near the new bike path that circles back to town.

Then Pepper and Belle wheel their bikes onto the path toward town and home. Behind them a car slows down, then speeds up and passes fast. They turn their heads back in time to see a small brown dog dash across the road into the wild rosebushes.

The girls call and search for the puppy in the thick brush. They hunt through the bushes for a long time trying to coax the dog out. Finally, they empty their boxes of raisins onto the ground, and leave bits of oatmeal cookie: then pick up their bikes and head for home.

Pepper and Belle go home and get tough work gloves and a set
of tools. They break down and move away the last pieces of
wood fence that separated the two doghouses of Rex and Ethel.

They nail these boards over and around the two old houses:
so two houses become one wide animal place in the middle
of one shared yard.

During these last days of August before the new school term begins,
the girls and their friends work on this animal place. They build
a bird feeder for redbirds and robins, and a squirrel station
loaded with black walnuts and ears of corn.

Suet balls hang for song sparrows. There are dishes of food for
stray cats and nighttime raccoon families. Fresh water drips
into a large bowl from a faucet that is always open.

At the back of the yard   the girls cut branches and pile them among
thick brush.   These piles will become new homes for rabbits and raccoons.
Soon there are many safe places   for possum   and groundhogs,
blue jays and doves.

Neighbor families help with saws and paint   until the work is finished.
A paint-fresh signboard is nailed above the new animal place.

The Rex and Ethel Memorial Rest Stop is this new wide house
filled with straw and pieces of old rug.

The Rex and Ethel   Memorial Rest Stop   is   opened   by Pepper and Belle
in   their   shared   yard.

One cooler morning   in early September,   Pepper and Belle
are waiting   at the corner of their street   for the first bus
for the first day of school.
They turn their heads in time to see their small puppy yap
her way out of the wide new house   and run along the clothesline lead
in   their   yard.
A redbird flies to the top branch of a tall black walnut tree,
and a squirrel on the ground   stops   still.

The puppy   begins to eat some breakfast food.
Redbirds   fly   down   to   their   feeder.
Squirrel   picks up a wrinkled   black   walnut
              and   zags   to   its   leafy   nest.

Pepper and Belle   get on their bus to school.

Another   day   begins.